Native American Cookbook

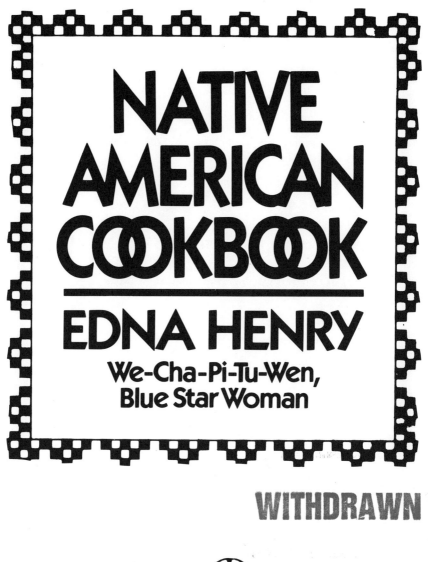

NATIVE AMERICAN COOKBOOK

EDNA HENRY

We-Cha-Pi-Tu-Wen, Blue Star Woman

Julian Messner New York

Text Copyright © 1983 by Edna Henry
Illustrations Copyright © 1983 by Nadema Agard

All rights reserved including the right of reproduction in whole or in part in any form. Published by Julian Messner, a Division of Simon & Schuster, Inc. Simon & Schuster Building, 1230 Avenue of the Americas, New York, New York 10020.

JULIAN MESSNER and colophon are trademarks of Simon & Schuster, Inc.

Manufactured in the United States of America

Design by Beverly G. Haw Leung, A Good Thing, Inc.

0-671-41896-3

Library of Congress Cataloging in Publication Data.

Dedicated to the memory of
Albert Michael Henry

Contents

Introduction

Once, in the very old days, long before any Europeans came to this land, a tribe that had a very poor harvest and hunting season sent a messenger to another tribe to ask for food. These two tribes were not on the best of terms, although they were of the same nation and stood together in the face of common enemies. But sharing food was a different matter. The tribe refused to give the messenger any food, and he returned empty-handed to his village.

The "Chief–Without–Food" was angered, and he sent a runner back with a threat of war. Upon hearing this threat, the "Chief–With–Food" and his advisors told the runner that they were not afraid of the "Chief–Without–Food," his warriors, or their attacks.

This went on for two days. Finally, the two tribes decided to go to war. But in order not to lose any warriors, the war was to be in the form of a challenge dance.

The two tribes lined up, facing each other across a clearing. One or two dancers from each tribe went to the front of the line and danced until the dancers from one side or the

other fell to the ground from exhaustion. When only one man was left standing, he picked as many men as he wanted from his tribe to join him. Then he challenged any man or men on the opposing side to dance, and he boasted about himself and his tribe.

This continued until only one man—the winner of the war—was left standing. The winner was from the "Tribe–Without–Food."

It seems that before the dance, the "Tribe–With–Food" had overeaten, just to keep from having food to give away if they lost the contest. They forgot that overeating would make dancing difficult.

Anyway, the dancers from *both* tribes were so tired that it wasn't until the next day that anyone could eat. Then a feast was prepared by the women of the "Tribe–With–Food" and they all celebrated, holding hands and dancing in one big circle and singing of the events of the "battle."

This story was passed down from generation to generation in my family and was told and retold at family gatherings, and now I am telling it to you.

Years ago, cooking was done over an open fire, either indoors or out. Fires were attended by the women and girls and had to be constantly watched, for a spark could set the whole village on fire. Most things in the village were made of wood, grass, and skins, that could be quickly destroyed by flames. So, much care was taken in tending the fires for cooking or drying meat and fish.

To cook, food was usually packed in tightly woven grass baskets or in clay pots. Water was added, then hot stones were placed in the containers to boil the water. As the food boiled, seasonings such as bear or deer fat, berries, and roots were added. When tender, the food was taken out of the baskets or pots to be served, and the leftover liquid was used for stews and soups.

Another way of cooking was to put the baskets or pots into pits in the ground that were lined with wet corn husks and leaves. Sometimes the food would be put directly into the lined pit instead of first being put into pots. Hot stones were placed on top of the food or the containers, then a covering of leaves and soil, and the food was left to steam overnight. Clams, fish, dried meat, corn, beans, dried fruits, berries, or potatoes could be cooked in this way.

The men and boys hunted for squirrel, deer, duck, opossum, woodchuck, wild turkey, and rabbit. Before the Europeans brought steel tools, blades made of flint, a very hard rock, were tied to wooden handles for butchering game. Large game, such as bear, deer, elk, moose, had to be skinned and cut up where they fell. They were too heavy to carry back to the village whole. Temporary camps of wigwams or tepees would be built if the hunt was far off. Eastern natives used cone-shaped wigwams that looked like tepees, made with long tree branches as support poles and layers of bark for covering a second set of poles on the outside. Plains natives used tanned animal skins as coverings for their cone-shaped tepees.

Back at the villages, the women cleaned the hides and cut the meat into strips for cooking or drying. Every part of an animal was saved for use. Feathers were kept for bedding and clothing. The tendons of the animals, tissue attaching muscle to bone and called *sinew*, were kept to be made into thread for sewing, or as strings for tying, and for bowstrings for arrows.

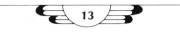

As a child, I would go out with the family to pick plants, roots, and berries. We would have a complete meal from the things we picked. Mother prepared the food we gathered. My mother was Nipmuc, from the northeast, but she prepared many dishes in the Tsárăgĭ (Cherokee) way because my father was Tsárăgĭ. Tsárăgĭ means "people of the caves" or "cave people" and was the ancient name given to people living in the northeastern part of North Carolina.

Mother always had a pot cooking on the back of the kitchen stove. The kitchen always smelled delicious, and was the center of all activities. Many people came, and we would dance and chant and tell stories and eat. This was like the old days, when a person could always find a kettle of some kind of food stewing in the middle of the village, easy for everyone to reach. In those days everybody brought their own eating utensils and sat on the ground to eat and tell stories and sing.

Today my friends and members of my family live as far apart as Alaska and the San Blas Islands off Panama, and from New York to Hawaii. But we still gather in one another's homes and at pow-wows and enjoy exchanging stories and recipes.

Here are some of them.

Some Native American Foods

In ancestral times, Native Americans depended on the richness of the earth to yield many foods. These foods were the colors of the earth—light brown, golden-brown, red-brown, and green. The earth colors in which they grow are echoed in yams, turnips, potatoes, and other roots and tubers. There is the tan of wheat, the gold and browns of corn, the greens of the leafy vegetables . . . .

Bleached or whitened ingredients, such as white flour and white sugar, don't have the colors of the earth and don't seem to taste as good as the wheat. For healthy color and good quality in your cooking, try cooking without them.

Some native ingredients are hard to find, so possible substitutes are indicated on the following pages.

NATIVE FOOD	SUBSTITUTES
acorn meal	corn or cracker meal, bread crumbs
apples, crab apples	
beans	
berries: sweet and acid buffalo berries and soapberries	acid: juniper berries, cranberries sweet: currants, blueberries, raisins, elderberries
black hardwood ashes	baking soda, baking powder
burdock leaves, used as vegetables (roots used as medicine)	
cattails	cornmeal, wheat or rye flour
coltsfoot leaves	salt
dandelion leaves as vegetable (roots for medicine)	kale, turnip tops
ground-up seeds	cracker-crumbs or breadcrumbs
hazel nuts, pine nuts, pecans, walnuts, peanuts, sunflower and pumpkin seeds	
lambs quarters (a green)	spinach, mustard greens
potatoes	
pumpkin	

NATIVE FOOD	SUBSTITUTES
maize—blue, red, or multicolored	yellow corn
maple syrup	brown sugar
milkweed	
saffron	saffron tea leaves
wild rice	rice
rape (plant of the mustard family)	
seaweed	salt
small birds' eggs	chicken eggs
squash, various types	
tomatoes	
wild celery	celery
wild garlic	garlic
wild leeks	leeks, onions, scallions
wild rice	brown rice
wild turnips	turnips
yams and sweet potatoes	

Some non-native labor-saving shortcuts like yeast and baking powder are given. Making breadstuffs rise without their help takes a lot of time and hard work. But try it sometime—you might enjoy it.

Ingredients marked with an asterisk (*) have also been added to original native recipes. Certain native dishes are quite bland and the ingredients have been added to give more flavor. Take them out or leave them in according to your own taste.

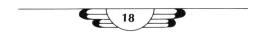

Basic Cooking Tools You Will Need

wooden cooking spoons, small and large

small, medium, and large saucepans, baking pans, oven roasters

two flat stones for crushing spices and herbs

sieves (strainers)

measuring cups and measuring spoons

knives

long-handled fork

aluminum foil

and—very important—your hands!

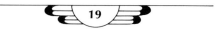

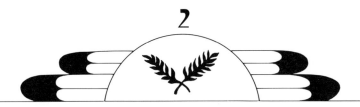

2

Maize (Corn)

In Cuba, the Taino natives called corn "mahiz." The Spanish who conquered Cuba called it "maiz," and in English the word became "maize." The Comanches called it Ch-Nee-Vee—(sounds like "honey bee").

The Europeans called their major cereal crops "corn." For instance, the English called wheat corn, and the Irish called oats corn. When Europeans came to America they called maize corn.

Various branches of the Algonquian Nation taught the Europeans who came to New England the art of planting corn: four grains to a tiny mound of dirt. Fish heads and seaweed were used to fertilize the soil.

The entire ear of corn was used, nothing was wasted. The kernels were eaten as a cereal or ground into a flour. The cobs were used to make a jelly. The husks were woven into baskets, mats, and trays or made into dolls for the children.

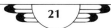

Hominy is kernels of corn with the outer skin removed. A Tsárăgĭ family made hominy by putting dried maize into a large kettle and soaking it in water with wood ashes from a Blackjack tree for an hour. This helped loosen the outer skin. Then they would scrub the corn with the ashes and work it quickly between the palms of their hands to shell the kernels. The kernels were boiled for thirty minutes. A long wooden paddle was used to stir the boiling kernels until the yellow husk was loosened or came off. The kernels were then washed in cold water, using a large container with nails in the bottom to scrape off the loose husks. The water was poured off and the washing process repeated. The result was hominy. Hominy looks like a swollen kernel of white corn. Dried hominy can be pounded into a grain called hominy grits.

Maize Soup

1½ cups dried kidney beans (or one can kidney beans)
½ cup hominy
½ cup maize/corn kernels
½ lb. smoked butt or fatback
1 bay leaf
1 small sliced onion, or two or three scallions
Water

1. Soak dried beans overnight in water to make them soft.
2. Put beans and fatback in a saucepan with enough water to reach about 2″ above beans. Cook for one ½ hour.
3. Add hominy and stir.
4. Cook for 15 minutes.
5. Add corn, stir.
6. Slice onion to make rings. Push out the rings of the onion and lay on top of mixture. Put bay leaf on top of onions and push under the liquid with a spoon.
7. Cook for about 20 minutes then take bay leaf out and stir well.
8. Cook for 1½ hours more.

Serve with corn bread, spoon bread, or Prince Albert bread. (See recipe page 54.)

Serves 6-8.

Tsaragi Yellow Maize Pudding

2½ cups corn kernels, cooked. (Cooked frozen corn, or drained canned corn can be used in place of fresh.)
½ cup brown sugar
1 teaspoon vanilla
2 eggs
1 cup evaporated milk
1 teaspoon cornstarch
½ teaspoon nutmeg
½ teaspoon cinnamon
Dash of salt
3 tablespoons butter or margarine

1. Place corn in saucepan.
2. Grease a 9″ round baking pan and set aside.
3. Melt butter in a small saucepan and set aside.
4. Mix sugar, nutmeg, salt, and cinnamon with corn.
5. Slightly beat eggs in a bowl.
6. Add eggs to corn mixture and stir well. Put over low heat and keep stirring until heated through.
7. Dissolve cornstarch in milk and add mixture to corn.
8. Add vanilla and melted butter. Stir well.
9. Pour into the greased baking pan and bake at 350° for 45 minutes. Test for doneness with a knife inserted in the middle. If knife comes out dry, the pudding is done. If not dry, continue cooking and test in 5 minutes.

Can be eaten as a potato substitute or dessert.

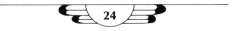

What To Do With The Leftover Maize From The Cobs

To make lovely maize necklaces, use ears of multi-colored corn. Remove kernels from the cob and boil in a saucepan until they are soft. Use a large needle and nylon fishing thread to string kernels. Hang to dry. Cut off as much as you want to make necklaces or bracelets. Re-knot strings.

3

The Nipmuc Way

Native Americans used turnips, parsnips, and carrots, which are roots, as vegetables. The Europeans who first came to New England refused to eat root vegetables and starved, although the natives showed them how to prepare these good foods.

In New England, the change from one season to another means a change of clothing, living conditions, and food to the Nipmucs. There are winter, spring, and summer Nipmuc stews.

The following recipe is from Princess White Flower of the Hassanamisco Reservation in Grafton, Massachusetts, where my aunts lived as children. Princess White Flower writes, "My dog and I live on this stew in the winter. It's inexpensive and easy to make. In the old days this stew lasted 'till spring. Usually roots and other meats were added along with squirrel, opossum, woodchuck, pheasant, partridge, duck or whatever meat was available."

Princess White Flower's Winter Stew

2 lbs. deer meat or beef
4-5 carrots
3-4 small onions
2 green peppers
1 stalk of leeks or green onions
3 cups meat stock or beef or chicken bouillon
1 clove garlic, smashed

1 basil leaf, crushed } mixed together
½ cup wheat germ   }

pepper to taste
1 tomato, or 1 cup tomato sauce
2 tablespoons oil

1. Marinate meat overnight in meat stock or bouillon.
2. Boil vegetables.
3. Cut meat in small bite-size pieces and roll pieces in wheat germ, garlic, basil mix. Brown meat in oil.
5. Add meat to vegetables. Simmer.
6. Add chopped leeks and tomato.
7. Simmer about two hours more, stirring occasionally, until tomato dissolves.

Leftover stew can be stirred, adding leftover vegetables from time to time, and adding a piece of meat when it's dinnertime.

DUMPLINGS (A later, non-traditional—but good—addition)

Biscuit mix
*¼ teaspoon curry powder

1. Make standard dumpling recipe with biscuit mix, adding curry powder.
2. Drop dumpling mix onto bubbling stew. Cook covered for 10 minutes and uncovered 10 minutes until dumplings are done.

Remove leftover dumplings when storing stew. They do not last as the stew does.

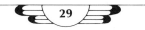

Okra, Corn, and Tomato Stew—
The Easy Way

1 can whole kernel corn
1 large fresh tomato or 12 oz. can stewed tomatoes
1 cup of cooked okra or 1 box of frozen okra
2 tablespoons flour
3 tablespoons bacon drippings
4-5 cooked bacon strips
3 cups water
Salt and pepper to taste.

1. Put corn with its liquid into a saucepan and add tomatoes and cleaned okra.
2. Add salt, pepper, and stir in flour.
3. Pour on the bacon drippings and add cooked bacon strips.
4. Cook until okra is tender, adding water as needed. Stew should be the thickness of a loose pudding.

Hassanamisco Fruit Bars or Spread

¼ cup maple sugar or dark corn syrup
½ cup water
1 cup mixed dry fruit and nuts cut up in very small pieces
½ cup apple or orange juice
Optional: 1 or more sheets of paper-thin seaweed (from Japanese foodstore)

1. Melt maple sugar in ¼ cup juice in a saucepan over low heat.
2. Add rest of juice, nuts, and fruit.
3. Simmer for ½ hour over low flame. The longer you simmer, the harder the mixture will get. If you want to use as a cake filling or topping, do not overcook, and you might try adding two raw eggs.
4. Spread over sheet of aluminum foil to cool.
5. To make candy bars, wrap by teaspoonful in 2" square pieces of seaweed. If seaweed is not used, simply sprinkle a little salt on mixture and cut into bars.

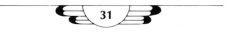

It's A Small World

My heritage is Nipmuc and Tsaragi, and I found a Tsaragi-style dish when I was living in Tokyo, Japan. It was not a Japanese dish, but an African one! I was invited to a consulate dinner by the first secretary of Ghana and was pleasantly surprised to learn that their native Ghanaian dish of peanut butter stew was very similar to a peanut soup prepared by the Tsaragi—the Cherokees.

As has happened so often in history when one culture meets another, something new results. In this case I blended two recipes to create this Ghanaian-Tsaragi stew.

Ghanaian—Tsaragi Peanut Butter Stew

3 lbs. stewing chicken, cut up
2 or 3 large cloves of garlic, crushed with stones.
1 medium onion, chopped
3 medium tomatoes, chopped
2 tablespoons oil, margarine, or butter
3 cups chicken bouillon or broth

½ cup whole peanuts } or 18 oz. chunky peanut
18 oz. peanut butter (smooth) } butter

12 oz. can tomato paste
15 oz. can tomato sauce
*3 or 4 dashes tabasco or hot sauce
salt and pepper to taste
4 or 5 cups water
Optional: papaya seeds to tenderize chicken

1. Place chicken in a large saucepan or kettle with garlic.
2. Add water to cover chicken (about 1″ above chicken).
3. Boil for 20 minutes then turn down to low heat and simmer for 2 hours.
4. Test the chicken to see if it is tender. When it is, add tomatoes and onion. Cook for 20 minutes more.
5. Add 3 cups of chicken bouillon or broth and stir.
6. Add salt, pepper, peanuts, peanut butter, tomato paste and tomato sauce, stirring well.
7. Cook on low flame until it begins to bubble.
8. Add tabasco or hot sauce.

Serves 6-8.

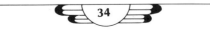

"Hey Turkey"

The turkey has been a part of the North, Central, and South American heritage for centuries. The Spanish first saw the turkey in Mexico, where the natives raised them. Turkeys were taken to Europe in the early 1500s and reintroduced by the Pilgrims in late 1620. However, New England already had many wild turkeys. The Pilgrims called their bird a "furkee."

Like most forest creatures, the turkey is well camouflaged. You cannot see him in the woods, if he stays put. The turkey is not quite so dumb as some people think, but he is a curious bird. He will stick his head up to investigate a noise and so get killed by a hunter. Sometimes turkeys will stare at their reflection in the water, fall in, and drown. "Hey, turkey!"

Turkey with Wild Rice Stuffing

1 small turkey—about 5-6 pounds (or large roasting chicken).

*2 cups chicken bouillon

½ cup wild rice

3 tablespoons butter or margarine or beef suet that has been rendered or melted down and then refrigerated so it is consistency of butter.

½ teaspoon crushed rosemary

½ teaspoon crushed thyme

½ teaspoon crushed oregano

½ teaspoon crushed dried garlic; or one clove fresh garlic, crushed with a stone and outer papery cover removed.

½ cup green pepper, chopped

1 small onion, chopped; or 2 tablespoons onion flakes

1 apple peeled, cored, and chopped (You can use ½ cup dried apples.)

½ cup raisins

Black pepper and salt (optional)

PREPARE TURKEY:

1. Rub 1 tablespoon butter, and salt and pepper chicken inside and out if you like.
2. Wrap loosely in aluminum foil, a modern stubstitute for leaves.
3. Cook in 350° oven about ½ hour for chicken, 1½ hours for turkey.

PREPARE STUFFING (while turkey is cooking):

1. Cook wild rice in 1½ cups bouillon or stock until tender.
2. When rice is cooked, put 2 tablespoons of butter, margarine, or fat into a frying pan and cook onion and green pepper for 1 minute.
3. Add herbs (rosemary, thyme, oregano) and crushed garlic. Mix well.
4. Cook 2 minutes, then add apples and raisins. Mix well.
5. Add the rest of the stock or bouillon (about ½ cup) and the wild rice. Mix well. Cook until all liquid has been absorbed. Let cool.

Pack stuffing loosely into bird. Return to oven to finish cooking—about 1½ hours for turkey, 1¼ hours if using chicken.

Serves 8.

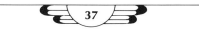

Wild Rice

Wild rice is not rice. It is a grain with a shape similar to rice. Like rice, it grows in muddy, watery areas. Wild rice has a purple-black color and an herbal taste. The Chippewa called it *Me-goo-ch Me-mo-men*, and used wild rice as a staple like bread or potatoes. The French called it *avoine folle*, "wild oats" or "crazy oats." The English explorers gave it the name "wild rice." Today wild rice is not so wild—it is cultivated, or specially grown—but it is wildly expensive.

To prepare:

1 cup wild rice
1 teaspoon salt
1 cup meat stock. Or one chicken or beef bouillon cube
dissolved in one cup of boiling water.

1. Wash rice in cold water. The rice must be washed well to get rid of some of the strong herbal flavor. Put the rice into an uncovered saucepan with the one cup of water and salt.
2. Bring to a fast boil, then reduce heat. Leave pot uncovered.
3. When all the water is absorbed, stir in the cup of meat stock or bouillon.
4. Cook gently until all liquid has been absorbed and rice is tender.

Serves 4 as a side dish.

Bonnie, Buck,
and the Baby

My cousin Bonnie is Tsaragi, married to a Hopi named Buck. Their baby is named Honey Bear.

My aunt taught Bonnie and me a chant that we sang when we were together. Buck would join in with his drum. Sometimes Honey Bear would take a feather, point towards the night sky and try to "baby chant" along with us. The chant went like this:

Old mother moon, what big eyes you have.
"You better be good, you better be good!"
High in the sky, someone's looking at you.
"You better be good, you better be good!"

On one of these occasions, Bonnie and Buck served a bowl of stewed greens and something that looked like black cobwebs. It was delicious. The taste of the greens was nothing I could identify so I asked them what it was. They laughed and said it was a mixture of greens and vaseline. Well, vaseline I know, but what kind of greens? They wouldn't say. What I thought were cobwebs was really corn piki bread, a very thin corn mixture spread on a hot block rock. The rock cooks the mixture, which is peeled off like tissue paper, giving the bread a cobweb appearance. Later, we all sat down to large bowls of chili and fry bread.

I never did learn the correct recipe for the stewed greens. It really was good. But . . . here is the recipe for the fry bread.

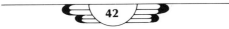

Fry Bread

5 cups whole wheat flour
1 tablespoon baking powder
1 teaspoon salt
¼ cup of milk or powdered milk
2 cups warm water
2 cups oil or shortening for frying

1. Mix flour, baking powder, and salt together in a large bowl.
2. Stir in water with a wooden spoon, then mix with hands until all the ingredients are blended. If too sticky to manage, add a little more flour.
3. Form dough into a ball and let stand a few minutes.
4. Pinch off a piece of dough the size of a lemon and roll into a small ball. Dust ball lightly with flour.
5. Pat ball down into a flat circle, like a pancake, then quickly flip back and forth between the palms of your hands so it thins and spreads until it is the size of a saucer. Set aside.
6. Heat two cups of oil or shortening in a saucepan.
7. Test oil to see if it is hot by dropping a pinch of dough in the oil—if the dough sizzles, the oil is ready.
8. Starting from the side of the saucepan farthest away from you, lay the dough down carefully so that it will lie flat on top of the oil. The dough will brown quickly and puff up. Turn the fry bread over with a long-handled fork and brown other side.
9. Remove from saucepan and place on paper towel to drain oil.
10. Repeat from step 4 until all dough is used up. Make sure oil does not get too hot. Test with a small piece of dough. If the test dough burns rapidly, take the pan off the heat for a minute or two.

Makes about 8 pieces.

Children's Tea

Called "Boys' Tea" by my grandmother, who gave the recipe to the family. In my family, boys were special, the tradition of my clan. But now we treat all our children as special. So "Boys' Tea" has become "Children's Tea." It is especially good before going to bed.

½ cup undiluted evaporated milk
½ cup hot water
2 teaspoons wild honey (any kind)
Dash of cinnamon

Mix all the above ingredients in a large cup.
Makes 1 serving. Multiply by number of children.

I-U Tea (Labrador Tea) or, in Alaska, Tundra Tea

Pull stems of dark green leaves growing on bushes and let dry upside down from a ceiling beam, on the wall, or in a closet. After one week the leaves should be dry. Pick off a handful and boil in a quart of water. Strain. Can be mixed with other tea. Sweeten with honey and drink hot.

7

The Shinnecocks and Narragansetts

Like the Nipmucs, The Mashpees, and the Pequots, the Shinnecocks of Long Island, New York are part of the Algonquian Nation.

Every year many Native American tribes gather with the Shinnecocks for a pow-wow in Southampton, Long Island. At this time everyone exchanges information and tales. During one of these gatherings the story was told that buckskin clothes were fringed to allow rain water to drain off so the buckskin body of the garment kept dry. Some said that the fringes imitated the long grasses when they blew back and forth in the wind.

Sometimes at these pow-wows we would walk along the shorelines looking for "paint pots," small stones which, when rubbed together, made a red coloring for our cheeks.

Shinnecock Succotash

2 cups of cranberry beans or pinto beans
1 cup corn kernels (small can whole kernel corn can be
  used)
2 fillets of fish (any kind of fish will do), cut crosswise
2 tablespoons of butter or margarine
1 teaspoon black pepper
1 bay leaf
¼ green pepper, diced
½ tomato, chopped
1 piece of seaweed (or a dash of salt)

1. Soak beans overnight in water to make them soft.
2. Put beans in a saucepan with water about 2″ above
   beans.
3. Cook over medium heat until beans are done, about
   2½ hours, adding water as needed to keep beans covered.
4. Add seaweed or salt, black pepper, fish, green pepper,
   and tomato. Stir gently.
5. Stir in butter or margarine.
6. Simmer for 15 more minutes.

Cattails

Cattails are a kind of water plant that can be found at the edges of streams or marshes. They can be easily recognized by their slender stems and fuzzy seed heads. Just about every part of them can be used.

In the spring, you can pick cattails when they are green and young. Peeled and boiled like corn on the cob, the seed heads have a squashlike taste.

In summer, cattails become brown and mature. They can be used to make biscuits, or can be added to soups, gravies, or hot cereals to thicken them. The cattail "potato," a growth on the root, can be put into a soup along with any shellfish, fish, or meat.

Cattail leaves can be brewed for a delicious tea or they can be soaked and woven, while wet, into mats and containers. This is a skill developed mainly by the Narragansetts, also of the Algonquian Nation, who come from Rhode Island, where many cattails grow.

Cattail Biscuits

6 whole cattails
½ cup yellow cattail pollen
1 cup cattail flour (see step 5 below)
1 tablespoon cornstarch
1 tablespoon baking powder (Baking powder is a modern addition—but a useful one.)
1 teaspoon salt

1. Shake pollen into a pot or saucepan and put aside.
2. Peel brown skin of root away and put root immediately into a bowl of water. You don't want the root to dry out.
3. Clean off root hairs and any white side shoots.
4. Slice roots lengthwise and put into a bowl of water.
5. To make the flour, take a bunch of the sliced roots in your hands and twist or mash, tearing apart a few at a time. This loosens the starchy flour from the fiber. When the fibers are stringy and the water is muddy-looking, start to pour off the water. You should see the cattail flour settle to the bottom as a sticky white substance. If flour has not settled, use a cheesecloth or other fine woven cloth when straining the water off. The flour will be left behind in the cheesecloth.
6. Put flour into pot with pollen and add salt and baking powder. Stir thoroughly. If you do not use baking powder, beat until mixture becomes bubbly with air and is shiny.

7. Blend very well with hands.
8. Powder hands with the cornstarch and roll a handful of mixture between your hands to make a ball. Mixture should make 4 to 6 balls.
9. Flatten the balls with your hands to about ½" thickness and put into a baking pan.
10. Bake at 400°F for about 15 minutes or until golden brown.

Eat with baked yams, bacon, pork, and bitter greens.

Carol's Candy

1½ cups of fresh peanuts, shelled
1 cup maple sugar
2 tablespoons butter

1. Combine all ingredients in small saucepan over low heat.
2. Stir constantly until mixture is thick—about 3 minutes. Mixture should be firm. If not, add more units.
3. Drop by wooden spoonfuls onto aluminum foil.
4. Let cool.

Makes six clusters if you use a big spoon, eight to ten with a small spoon.

Bread Dessert

2 slices of stale or toasted bread
2 tablespoons honey
Peelings from one apple, cut up
2 tablespoons currants
1 teaspoon lemon juice

1. Heat honey until soft in a medium-sized saucepan.
2. Add peelings and currants. Stir over low flame.
3. Crumble bread and add a little at a time to saucepan.
4. Stir until all the honey is absorbed by the bread and ingredients are evenly distributed throughout.

Can be eaten as is or with milk like a cereal.

My Mixture

Handful of raisins
Handful of shelled pumpkin seeds
Handful of shelled sunflower seeds

Mix all together in a bowl and eat with fingers like candy.

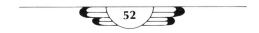

Sweet Stuff

Sweet stuff is made by mixing dry stuff with wet stuff.

DRY STUFF

2 cups cracked or rolled whole wheat flour
2 cups old-fashioned-style oatmeal
½ cup unsalted peanuts
½ cup raw cashews
½ cup coconut
1 tablespoon salt
¼ cup sesame seeds
1 cup sunflower seeds
1 cup wheat germ

1. Combine all these ingredients in a large bowl and blend with your hands.
2. Prepare wet stuff.

WET STUFF

1 cup vegetable oil
1 cup honey

1. Warm honey until soft.
2. Blend oil and honey until creamy.
3. Pour wet stuff into dry stuff.
4. Mix all together in the bowl.
5. Spread this on a large pan or cookie sheet.
6. Toast 200-300° in the oven for 30 minutes.
7. Stir often to brown evenly until crisp, but not too dark.

Can be eaten with milk, raisins, apples or any other fruit.

8

The Iswa (Catawba)

The Catawbas were also known as *Esaw* or *Issa* by many people who couldn't pronounce the name *Iswa* correctly. *Iswa* means "river" and the Iswa lived along the Santee and Wateree Rivers and the streams that fed into them in North and South Carolina. The Iswa are of Siouan stock and were the most important Eastern Siouan tribe along with the Tsárăgĭ, the Crows, the Dakotas, and the Mandans. *Catawba* comes from *Katapa*, a name probably given to the Iswa by the Choctaws and meaning "divided" or "separated."

Recipes were passed up and down the far reaches of the rivers from village to village. Young hunters brought deer, medicine plants, and lots of wild onions and other vegetables into the camps for trading.

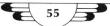

During one of these long trips downstream, a group of hunters found newcomers at a neighboring village. The new people were wearing strange clothes, speaking in an odd language, and were not a brown color like the Catawba. The hunters were wary, but there were cousins from other villages in the camp so it seemed safe to go in.

In the camp there was a great deal of activity, much hand-waving, pointing, and showing of articles. The newcomers and the natives were bargaining! Bargaining, however, was fun and enjoyed by the young hunters. After their business was done, the hunters exchanged food secrets with the strangers and gave them many recipes for preparing pumpkins. The newcomers showed everyone how to use baking soda and other ingredients to make dough rise.

With this new knowledge, the young men returned upstream to their village, and many generations to come passed on the story of this trip and the recipes exchanged that day. This next recipe is one of them. It is called Prince Albert Pumpkin Bread.

Prince Albert Pumpkin Bread

3 cups sifted whole wheat flour
1 tablespoon baking soda
1 tablespoon sea salt or table salt
3 tablespoons cinnamon
2 cups brown sugar
2 cups pumpkin (or 1 lb. can)
½ cup crushed pecans or walnuts (use stones to crush)

1. Place all ingredients in a large bowl.
2. Mix with a wooden spoon. Let rest for at least 20 minutes—the longer the better.
3. Preheat oven to 350°.
4. Prepare two loaf pans by buttering the insides using your fingers.
5. Make a deep well in the center of the pumpkin mixture and pour into the well:

   2 eggs, beaten
   1 cup corn oil or vegetable oil
   few raisins or juniper berries
6. Stir just enough to mix well.
7. Pour into the two buttered loaf pans and bake for one hour.

9

The Seminoles

Catawba is a name meaning "separated" in Choctaw and the name *Seminole* is Creek for "separate" or "runaway." Before 1775, some Creeks, other native American peoples, and Africans banded together and went south to Florida to escape slavery and warring tribes. The descendants of these groups are called *Seminoles*.

When the Spanish ruled Florida, they influenced the Seminole manner of dress by introducing European fabrics. Overhunting made deer skins used for clothing scarce so the Seminoles substituted Spanish fabrics. The Seminole women pieced together many different fabrics in a kind of patchwork. The men wore patchwork shirts that often extended to their knees. The women wore long skirts with colorful patterns circling the hem, and thin, short capes that were usually transparent. The capes protected them from insects but the women were able to keep their bodies cool in the Florida heat and humidity. However, with the arrival of Christian missionaries, the Seminole women were forced to cover up by wearing blouses under their sheer capes.

Fish has always been an important Seminole food because Florida is almost completely surrounded by water, and has many inland lagoons, rivers, and lakes.

Fruit and Fish Seminole Style

1 fillet of any solid type of fish
3 tablespoons fresh lemon juice
2 oranges, broken into sections
Butter
Salt and pepper to taste

1. Place orange slices on top of the fish.
2. Sprinkle 3 tablespoons lemon juice over fish and dot with 4 pieces of butter.
3. Wrap in aluminum foil and bake or broil for 45 minutes at 400° F. (Or use large leaves or seaweed to wrap as the natives did.)

Serves 2.

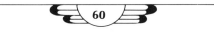

Seminole Drink

1 8-ounce glass of orange juice (1 can— 8 ounce—orange juice or orange drink can be used.)
3 oranges, sectioned (or 1 small can of orange sections)
3 diced pimentos
*2 teaspoons of spicy hot sauce

1. Put oranges and pimentos into bowl.
2. Pour in orange liquid.
3. Stir in hot sauce to taste.
4. Refrigerate. Serve cold, but do not use ice cubes.

Serves 1 or 2.

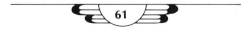

10

The Cuna Natives of the San Blas Islands

The San Blas Islands are located along the Republic of Panama's Caribbean coast. The islands are occupied by the Cuna natives.

In Cuna society, unlike most Native American groups, daughters are preferred to sons. The line of inheritance of a family is through the women and not the men. Unless a new husband can present his wife's family with a large dowry or gift, he must work for several years for his new family.

In the early part of the 1700s the Cuna women were hidden by their men from the Spanish explorers and other European men. Cuna women painted their bodies in bright colors. This was offensive to the religious beliefs of the Europeans. But the women could not be hidden forever, and eventually body painting was stopped. The Cuna women transferred their delight in bright colors to the making of *molas*, an embroidered covering worn from the waist to the knee. Under the mola was a painted cloth called a *picha makkalet*. Today, colorful trade cloth has

replaced the picha, and the mola has been shortened and raised to blouse length. Many Cuna women wear trade cloth or a mola draped over their heads, tight red bead work around their ankles and wrists, and a gold ring in their noses.

Molas are made from layers of fabric, each a different color. The design is cut through until the desired colors are reached in the lower layers. Then the outlines of the cut work are sewn down. Embroidery is used for details such as eyes, claws, whiskers, or finishing off the work. Sometimes it takes from six to eight months to make one side of a mola. Girls as young as seven or eight are taught by their mothers to make these molas—and to cook.

Plantains are used a lot in Caribbean cooking, and therefore in Cuna cooking. Plantains are like bananas. When very ripe and almost black, they are very sweet. Peeled, sliced, and fried, they are delicious served with chicken and rice, or beans and rice, or mashed with milk.

When they are green, plantains are not sweet. But they are very good peeled, floured, fried and eaten like potatoes. Here is a Cuna recipe for a stew that is made with plantains.

San Blas Stew

2 green plantains
2 peeled medium yellow yams, scrubbed and jackets left on
1 chicken (cut-up)
*½ teaspoon saffron or 2 tablespoons tomato paste or 2 tablespoons of saffron flowers used as tea
4 cups water
½ cup fresh coconut or one package of unsweetened coconut
Salt to taste

1. Boil yams and plantains in 4 cups of water on high flame until water begins to boil, then turn down to a low flame.
2. Put in chicken and coconut, stir to mix.
3. Cook with cover on for 1½ hours until meat is tender. Add saffron.
4. Uncover pot and let stew bubble and thicken.

The word *saffron* comes from the Arabic word *za'faran*, meaning yellow. Saffron was brought to the Americas by the Spaniards, who got it from the North Africans. The native Americans in contact with the Spaniards learned to use saffron often. They sometimes called it "hay." Saffron grows in loosely matted patches of dark red or golden orange flowers. Saffron stigmas, three thin rods inside the flower, have an iodinelike odor and taste when dried, but

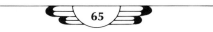

this is not overwhelming when added to foods. Saffron is very expensive. It takes about 12,000 stigmas from 4,000 flowers to make *one ounce* of saffron. The flowers are used for tea and are much less expensive. Saffron tea can be bought in a health store.

11

The Southwest

The Squash Blossom

In 1528 or 1529, a Spanish expedition to Florida led by Cabeza deVacas was shipwrecked along the Gulf Coast of present-day Texas and Louisiana. The men spent about eight years wandering through forest, mountains, and desert of what is now Arizona and New Mexico, seeking fellow Spaniards.

Only four survivors were left when they found their way to Mexico. But in Mexico they were taken prisoner by the natives. One of the four was a man named Estevanico. He was a Spanish Moor whose ancestors were from North Africa, and he was said to have magical powers. Those powers earned him the rank of shaman (medicine man) even while he was a captive.

When Estevanico and the others were freed, they took stories back to Spain of native cities of great wealth.

Explorer-missionary Friar Marcos de Niza went to the Southwest in 1539 with Estevanico as a guide and interpreter. Advancing ahead of the party, Estevanico and some Mexican natives, probably from the Mayan nation, reached Halona or Hawikuh, a Zuni city.

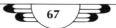

Estevanico was an impressive sight, riding into Halona with a greyhound dog running beside his horse. The Spaniard was decorated with feathers all over his clothing, making him look like a huge bird. Around his wrists and ankles hung bells, making musical sounds as he rode. Around his neck he wore a jeweled crescent and eye, the symbol of the Moslem Moors.

Estevanico's bearing and appearance impressed the Zuni, and his ability to speak their language enabled him to act as a go-between or ambassador for Friar de Niza. But Estevanico became too sure of himself. He displayed a gourd rattle he had saved from his earlier wanderings in the desert. This was recognized by the Zunis as a sacred object from another tribe. Angered by Estevanico's casual use of the rattle, or exasperated by the Spaniards' demands, the Zunis released a flight of arrows at Estevanico and his Mexican native companions. Estevanico was killed.

Alarmed by Estevanico's death, Friar de Niza fled back to Mexico with the rest of his party. At the top of a hill he looked back at the city of Halona. In the setting sunlight, the roofs reflected rays off the rocks, making them look like gold. This convinced the friar that this was one of the Seven Cities of Gold of Zuni legend and rich with treasures. Many more Spanish expeditions followed, but they found no cities of gold.

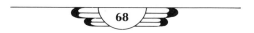

The Zunis, however, learned beautiful silverwork from the Spanish. One of the designs they used was Estevanico's Moorish crescent and eye. The design is used to this day in Native American silverwork and is part of the well-known squash blossom necklace. The squash blossom necklace is composed of three parts: the bead, the crescent, and the trumpet. The trumpet was designed from the blossom of the squash plant, and gives the necklace its name.

Squash blossoms are not only pretty enough to be designs for jewelry, they also make very good eating.

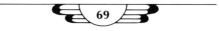

Stuffed Squash Blossoms

10 or more squash blossoms (Male blossoms are preferrable because they are larger.)
1 whole chicken, boiled
or 1 lb. ground meat, pan fried
½ cup bread crumbs
½ cup crushed nuts (fresh or unsalted canned hazelnuts or peanuts)
1 cup chopped mushrooms (fresh or canned)
½ cup evaporated milk
Chicken broth or bouillon, as needed to moisten

1. Let chicken cool. Shred meat from bones.
2. Put all ingredients in a bowl and mix well.
3. Open each squash blossom flower and fill with mixture. Do not overfill—the petals of each blossom must be able to close again.
4. Place blossoms side by side in a greased baking dish.
5. Bake in a moderate oven (350°) until tender and light brown, about 20 minutes.

Serves 5.

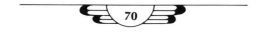

Baked Summer Squash

2 or 3 large summer squashes
2 tablespoons butter, melted ⎫
⎬ mixed
3 teaspoons lemon juice ⎭
1 teaspoon paprika
½ cup milk
Salt to taste
Small amount of cracker or bread crumbs

1. Cut squash into strips, lengthwise.
2. Place in a greased baking dish.
3. Add lemon-butter mixture and milk.
4. Sprinkle squash with paprika and salt.
5. Bake until tender (about ½ hour).
6. Add a sprinkling of cracker or bread crumbs.

Serves 4-6.

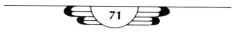

Stuffed and Baked Squash

4 small young summer squashes, cut down the middle
  lengthwise. (Skin should not be removed.)
2 tablespoons butter or margarine
2 tablespoons chopped onions
½ cup grated mild cheese
½ teaspoon salt
Dash of saffron or paprika
Dash of nutmeg or cloves
1 beaten egg

1. Cook onions in a little butter until transparent. Set
   aside.
2. Scoop out pulp of squash, leaving about ½" pulp in
   shell.
3. Rub shells with butter or margarine.
4. Add remaining ingredients *except* egg to pulp. Cook
   until hot.
5. Add beaten egg to mixture and mix through quickly.
6. Fill squash shells with mixture and bake in 350° oven
   until tender, about 25 minutes.

Serves 8.

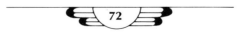

Jerky

Jerky was used by hunting tribes and European explorers, trappers and settlers on long trips and in the winter when fresh food was scarce. It is a name given dried meat or fish by mountainmen because of the way it had to be pulled and jerked from the teeth as they chewed.

Jerky is made from deer (venison), buffalo, elk, caribou, moose, or beef. The meat was first soaked in a mixture of salt and water (brine), then dried over a small fire. A hickory wood fire is preferred for it helps to keep the insects away and also flavors the meat. It is better to make jerky when it is windy. The wind helps keep the flies away from the meat. A straw mat or cloth is used at night as a cover.

Jerky was eaten "as is" or made into stews or soups or pemmican. To make pemmican, the jerky was pounded into tiny pieces, then berries, wild greens, or herbs were added for flavoring. Some melted fat was added, but not too much, since fat became rancid and could spoil the taste. Suet, spices, and apples added to the pemmican made mincemeat.

Strips of dried smoked salmon were once called "squaw candy." "Squaw" is an unpleasing word to native American women. So if you are unable to say Ee-Say-Tsit, meaning "smoked narrow fish," or Pah-Nee-Tuk, meaning "dry fish," in the Inupiat language, then say "smoked salmon strips". We will like you for it.

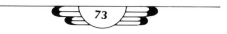

Meat Jerky

2 lbs. flank, round, or lean chuck steak, semi-frozen so it is
   easy to cut into thin slices.
1 cup water
1 teaspoon coarse salt
1½ teaspoons Liquid Smoke (modern ingredient to give
   taste of wood fires)
*¼ cup soy sauce
1 teaspoon onion powder
½ teaspoon garlic powder
½ teaspoon ground black pepper
*Dash of Tabasco

1. Cut away fat from meat.
2. Mix all ingredients except meat in a bowl.
3. Slice meat in thin, long strips lengthwise along the
   grain, then put the meat strips into the mixture and let
   sit for two hours.
4. Hang strips from rack in oven. Set oven at 200° or
   lowest temperature. Leave oven door slightly open.
   When strips become hard, dry, and black, they are
   ready—about 24 hours.
5. For larger amounts, do not marinate. Hang strips on
   thin poles and leave in the sun. Keep dry—cover if the
   weather is threatening. Or hang strips in the attic. This
   will take about two weeks to dry properly, depending
   on the weather. This is how it was done in the old
   days.

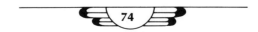

Fish Jerky

Split fish open, bone, and hang lengthwise on poles to dry. Or follow the same oven drying method as for meat jerky.

Old-fashioned Pemmican

Pound up a quantity of jerky. Then cut raw animal fat into walnut-size hunks. Melt in a pan in the oven or over a slow fire, never letting the grease boil up. Pour the resulting hot fat over the shredded jerky, mixing the two together thoroughly until you have the consistency of a sausage. Then pack the pemmican in casings of cleaned intestines. Add dried berries to suit yourself.

—or—

1. Pound jerky into a powder.
2. Fry some suet (beef, deer, or moose fat). Take out suet that doesn't melt and put aside.
3. Spoon a little hot melted grease into powdered jerky — just enough to make mixture workable. Add some bone marrow to help hold it together. Mix.
4. Cut up the cooked suet into small pieces and add to mixture. Squeeze together.
5. Add dried berries if you want. Acid berries (soapberries, buffaloberries, elderberries) help keep down the development of bacteria and slow down spoilage rate.
6. Squeeze into balls.
7. Let balls dry out a little before eating.

The amount of jerky powder will determine how many balls you will have.

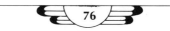

Modern Pemmican Balls

As made by some native families on the East Coast today.

1 small box dry mincemeat
¼ cup raw suet
1 or 2 teaspoons melted fat
½ cup jerky, pounded into powder or pieces

1. Fry raw suet until it is brown and well done.
2. Put mincemeat in a bowl.
3. Use a blender if you have one, setting on "crumbs" or "chop," to cut up jerky. If you don't have a blender, cut up jerky with scissors into very small pieces, or use stones to break up the jerky.
4. Add fried suet and jerky to mincemeat.
5. Squeeze into balls, the size of golfballs.
6. Let the balls dry out before eating.

Sioux (La-Ko-Ta) Foods

Some Sioux words for foods:

Ta-Tan-Ka	=	Buffalo
Wa-Ga-Me-Za	=	Corn
Tah-Ca	=	Deer
Papa Sa-Ka	=	Dried meat (beef, moose, elk), or jerky
Wa-Sa-Na Papa	=	Dessert made with Papa
Wo-Ja-Pi	=	Mixed stew
Wa-Ga-Moo	=	Pumpkin, squash, cucumber
Wa-Ha-Pi	=	Soup
Ta-Nee-Ga	=	Intestines (beef, buffalo) used as casing for meat fillings
Teem-chay-La	=	Turnips
Wasté	=	Good

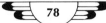

Wa-Ha-Pi Papa Sa-Ka La-Ko-Ta

1 cup Papa Sa-Ka
1 cup Wa-Ga-Me-Za
2 sliced **Teem-chay-La**
3 cups water
Dash of salt

1. Break up papa into a saucepan with water. Cook 15 minutes.
2. Stir in Wa-Ga-Me-Za and cook for 20 minutes.
3. **Teem-chay-La** must be boiled in water to lose their bitter taste. Change water and boil again if still a little bitter. Then slice and add to the pot. Cook 45 minutes to 1 hour.
4. Salt to taste.

Wasté (pronounce it wash-tay) with rice.

To make Wa-Sa-Na Papa, leave out Wa-Ga-Me-Za and Teem-Chay-La, and add 1 cup of berries.

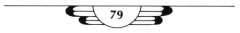

13

The Klondike

The natives along the Yukon River called the embankments a word that to the Europeans sounded like "Klondike," so the whole area was called the Klondike when the search for gold exploded there. To the Athapascans the word simply meant "the banks along the river," something like a palisade, where there was good fishing.

The following is a recipe given to me by my adopted grandfather from Beaver, Alaska, who experienced the hunt during the great Gold Rush days along the Klondike.

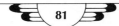

Toot-Too (Caribou) Flour Stew

1 lb. of Toot-Too meat, or beef, cut up
2½ cups water
1 cup wheat flour
1 medium onion, peeled and cut into pieces

1. Simmer meat and onion in a saucepan until tender.
2. Mix water and flour until smooth, pour over meat.
3. Stir over low heat until stew is thick.

Here are two other Klondike favorites.

Fry Silver Salmon

4 slices of silver salmon
1 cup evaporated milk
1 egg, beaten
2 tablespoons liquid fat or oil
1 cup wheat flour

1. Mix milk and egg together in a shallow dish and add fish, keeping pieces separate.
2. Pierce fish with fork, turn over and pierce other side.
3. Do this twice, then leave to soak in egg/milk mixture ½ hour.
4. Remove pieces from bowl and dust with wheat flour on both sides.
5. Fry in fat or oil until brown.

Serves 4.

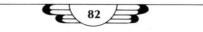

Red Salmon and Rice Supper

1 cup cooked rice (use directions on box)
1 teaspoon salt
*1 tablespoon curry powder
4 tablespoons butter or margarine
1 onion, chopped
2 stalks celery
½ cup milk
2 cups cooked fresh red salmon, or canned salmon, or
  any other fish
1 tablespoon lemon juice

1. In a frying pan, melt butter or margarine.
2. Add onion and celery.
3. Cook over low heat until celery and onion are tender.
4. Stir the onion and celery mixture into the rice.
5. Add milk, fish, lemon juice, and curry.
6. Heat over low heat for 10 minutes.

Serves 4.

by Angelo A. Allen

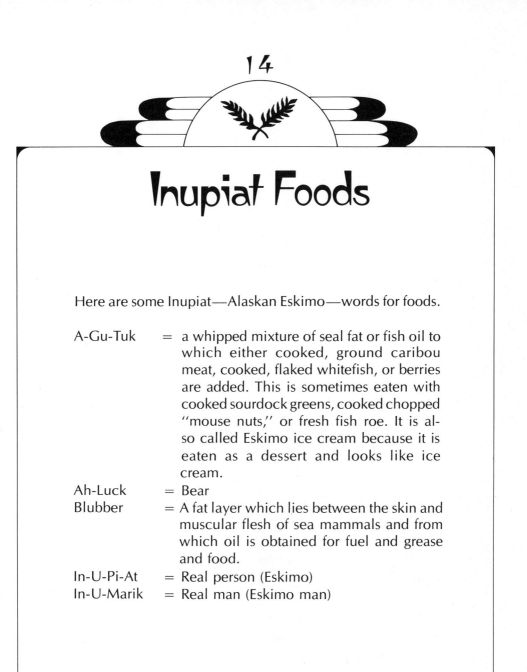

14

Inupiat Foods

Here are some Inupiat—Alaskan Eskimo—words for foods.

A-Gu-Tuk = a whipped mixture of seal fat or fish oil to which either cooked, ground caribou meat, cooked, flaked whitefish, or berries are added. This is sometimes eaten with cooked sourdock greens, cooked chopped "mouse nuts," or fresh fish roe. It is also called Eskimo ice cream because it is eaten as a dessert and looks like ice cream.

Ah-Luck = Bear

Blubber = A fat layer which lies between the skin and muscular flesh of sea mammals and from which oil is obtained for fuel and grease and food.

In-U-Pi-At = Real person (Eskimo)

In-U-Marik = Real man (Eskimo man)

K-Wak	= Frozen raw meat or fish.
Muk-Luk	= Southwestern Inupiat word for the large bearded seal. Also the name given to the snow boots using the tanned skins for soles.
Muk-Tuk	= The outer skin and attached layer of blubber of baleen and beluga whales. Eaten like candy.
Oo-Gruk-	= Seal
Pic-Nic	= 'Mouse nuts,' so-called because they are bits of edible roots and parts of tundra plants collected by rodents and buried underground to serve as food during the long cold winter.
Seal Poke	= The skin of the seal with the head and insides removed. The skin is turned inside out, cleaned, and blown up like a paper bag. It is dried, then returned to the hair side. The poke is used for storing berries, meats, roots, and other foods for the winter.
Sue-Wok	= Dried salmon eggs. Good with berries.
Tee-Nee-Ka	= Moose
Toot-Too	= Caribou

If you think fish eggs, seaweed, and blubber of whale are strange foods, then think of what people of other countries eat, and they won't seem so strange. The Arabs eat sheeps' eyes, the French eat frogs' legs and cat stewed in sherry is a favorite with Basque laborers in Spain.

Aged meat and fish are favorite foods among the Inupiat, especially among the older people who have eaten this since childhood. Food is stored in boxes and buried in the ground and left until it is runny. Instead of boxes some people have been using plastic wrap. But gases and bacteria build up in the plastic and cannot escape as the cracks in boxes allow. Some people have been poisoned, some have even died. So the old way of preparing foods is still the best way in some cases, and a campaign is being conducted to make the old people understand this.

An Inumarik Story

Dry salmon, frozen white fish with seal oil to dip it in, herring eggs on seaweed, fried smelts, and muk-tuk to nibble on makes good eating.

After such a meal we would sit around and tell stories. One day I was a guest in a home where the grandfather told a story about a hunt he went on as a little boy with his father. This is his story. In the Inumarik way he refers to himself as *"this man,"* never "I" or "me." In the old days this was a sign of humility.

This man was hunting one day far away from the village with the father. A polar bear came in view, but this day was for seals. So we did not go close but circled around the bear. If cubs were near the polar bear, this would be a very dangerous time, but there were no cubs. The ice this man traveled on was soft in some places with many holes we could fall through, and we were careful where to step. After looking much, we found seals. My father took his stick, poked

holes in the ice and this man helped poke many holes in the ice to make a slush. Then the father sat a long time at one hole, hidden behind a snow hill so that the seal would not see him or his shadow. When the seal saw a bright spot in the ice, he stuck his nose up through the hole to breathe, and the father drove the harpoon into him. The father worked very fast. He pulled on the line that tied the point to the harpoon shaft so that he could use the point again. We held firm to the line as the seal sank. Then my father and this man pulled the seal up on the ice. After this, we went to another hole for more seal. We had little daylight left so we returned to the village. For the night meal, we had oo-gruk and muk-tuk. Some muk-tuk was stored in seal pokes to be used later. We put some in a box and buried it in the ground or in a warm place so it would become runny and sour—seal oil, salmon cheese, and soured seal liver is made this way. Then the oo-gruk flippers were cut off, put in fresh blubber and left to stay for about three weeks so the hair would loosen and we could pull it off to eat the meat. This is a story of an Inumarik hunt.

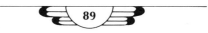

Real Agutak Ice Cream

1 cup caribou tallow, moose fat, or beef suet, melted
1 cup oo-gruk oil
½ cup of water or snow
3 cups crowberries or low bush cranberries
3 cups blueberries
1 cup white sugar (optional)

1. Pour small amount of oo-gruk oil slowly into the melted fat, whipping at the same time with your hands.
2. Add water and continue to whip.
3. Whip in the rest of the oil and water, a little at a time until mixture is white and fluffy.
4. Stir in sugar and berries.

Another Ice Cream

2 cups second day clean fallen snow
Sugar or honey and vanilla to taste
Berries if desired

Mix all ingredients together in bowl.

Serves two.

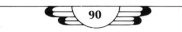

Modified Agutak Ice Cream

2 egg whites
½ cup vegetable oil, butter, or margarine
1 can tuna fish or any cooked fish
2 tablespoons vanilla
Brown sugar or honey to taste
Berries, if wanted

1. Separate egg whites from yolks. This is best done by carefully cracking an egg around the middle. Open the egg so the yolk sits in one half of the shell. Spill white out into bowl, then move yolk to other half of shell, spilling out more white. Move yolk back and forth until the white is all in the bowl. Beat egg whites with a beater until stiff and fluffy.
2. In another bowl put oil, then spoon in egg whites, a little at a time and mix.
3. Add vanilla, brown sugar, or honey.
4. Mix in fish.
5. Add berries if desired.

Serves two.

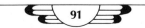

INDEX